Survival of the Fittest

A Warriors Guide to Victory

By Jennifer Moon

Survival of the Fittest

Jennifer Moon

Graphis Designs by Brian Hampton

Copyright © 2024

All Rights Reserved

ISBN: 9798335358347

Imprint: Independently published

All biblical text that is quoted in this book was quoted out of the King James Version Bible.

Dedication

I would like to thank the late Pastor Joe Cox for encouraging me to dig and find the message this book has to offer. I also would like to thank Pastor Justin Owens for encouraging me to pursue this gifting. Much appreciation to all who have played a part in causing me to step out of my comfort zone and put a dream into reality.

Endorsements

I endorse this book by Prophet Jennifer Moon as a survival guide for inner healing. The strategic plan of walking through healing from the beginning to the end has been expressed through her writing. It is a must read and one that you can use as a reference to go back to when needed. Jennifer has outlined the scriptures clearly throughout this book and it all has come forth with clarity.

Apostle Jennifer Leigh Butler

This is an amazing read. Every sentence will capture you and make you want more. You will not want to put it down. Prophet Jennifer Moon is a phenomenal writer that speaks from the heart of God!

Apostle Brian Hampton

Table of Contents

Introduction

There is a time coming when we are going to have to rely on our knowledge of the word and the Power of the Holy Ghost to live a healthy life. The word provides for us instances where God has naturally and supernaturally provided for His people. We need to be able to understand them and understand how to apply the scripture to our lives so that we may see deliverance through these times. The word brings life and healing, and our faith is activated through the study and application of the word. Proverbs 2:1-4 says, "My son if thou wilt receive my words, and hide my commandments with thee; So that thou incline thine ear unto wisdom and apply thine heart to understanding; Yea if thou criest after knowledge, and liftest up they voice for understanding; If thou sleekest her as silver searchest for her as for hid treasures." Inside the scriptures is everything we need to make it through this next level of our lives and all we must do is seek after God for the understanding of the word and the guidance in application of it.

Today man has made us dependent on their science and their medicine when all we really needed was the presence of God in our lives and the scriptures to contend with things that come against us in this life. Jesus said He is the bread of life, the light of the world, and the great physician. He provided food with five loaves and 2 fish, He forgave sin for deliverance of sickness, He cast out demons to save the person who was afflicted and diseased by them, He cleansed those who were considered unclean and troubled with an unclean spirit and healed the blind so that God would get the glory. John 14:12 says, "Verily verily I say unto you He that believeth on me, the works that I do shall he do also; and greater works than these shall he do; because I go unto my Father." He makes intercession for us that we might be able to walk in this authority and see these things unfold. But without understanding how else will we see that which He stated should happen?

Understanding

God is a God that honors his word so many times
our healing and our deliverance is in the simple act
of speaking His word back to Him in prayer
requesting that those same words be applied to our
lives. Isaiah 55:11 says, "So shall my word be that
goeth forth out of my mouth; it shall not return
unto me void, but it shall accomplish that which I
please, and is shall prosper in the thing whereto I
sent it." The word was written so that we can speak
it back to the Lord and cause Him to move. Our
obedience in study and understanding it is honored
by God through His honoring His word when we
speak it. In Ephesians the armor of God is listed as
being Prayer, truth as our belt, righteousness as our
breastplate, the preparation of the gospel as our
shoes, faith as our shield, helmet is our salvation,
and the only offensive weapon we have is the
SWORD of the spirit which is the word of God. It
is also our solid foundation which is why we have
to shod our feet with it. If we are not standing on
the word in battle then we have not solid
foundation and can be knocked down. When we
say stand, we must stand with these things in place
and know that God is one who has to honor those
who are being obedient to His word; and applying

the principles and teaching of it to their lives. We have to speak it back to Him not because he is not able to preform and move without our spoken word but it is because what we speak is what happens in our lives. There is power in the spoken word that is why James teaches us to bridle our tongue. He was speaking of blessing God with the same mouth that we use to speak curses on man in James 3:9-12. In Proverbs we find why he said that. Proverbs 18:21 says, "Death and life are in the power of the tongue; and they that love it shall eat the fruits thereof." James was saying we cannot be speaking life and death at the same time. That is why when we pray for a cleansing the first thing, we need to pray is for the God above to cleanse our thoughts and our tongue so that we are not speaking curses and blessings out of the same mouth. James 1:8 says "A double minded man is unstable in all his ways." What comes out of our mouth reflects what is in our heart and mind. God will judge our idle words and those curses that we speak about and too people is what stops the power of our tongue for the healing and deliverance we are asking God for.

The three-cord strand is not easily broken. Eccl. 4:12. So when we are looking at healing's deliverance and provision from God, we must focus on righteous living through repentance daily, constant fellowship and relationship with God, and continued worship. Those 3 things are the key to a life that will set you apart in Gods eyes and require Him to give attention to you when you call out to Him. If we are doing those three things our walk with God will be unbreakable through any attack.

Repentance

Therefore, we have to pray for sanctification and repent daily so we ourselves have no unrepented sin and uncleanness in us when we seek God for healing and deliverance. As Paul teaches in 1 Cor. 15:31 that he dies daily. This means that he repents daily for sins committed in order to grow and walk closer with God. He also teaches in Gal. 5:24 he says we must crucify our flesh. This means that we must continuously stay in repentance and seeking after Gods will in order to get our flesh to line up with the word of God. This type of living is required in order to be able to speak God's word and He be obligated to honor it. Which refers to the breast plate of righteousness and the helmet of salvation. The accuser Satan will create doubt with the blame and guilt he places on you if you attempt to pray and not be in right standing with God. The doubt is going to hinder your faith for the healing to take place.

Prayer

Constant fellowship with God comes from prayer. Again, part of the armor we are given for battle. Prayer is a defensive tool given to us, but it is also the way we communicate with God. 1 Thes.5:17 says to pray without ceasing. Now that does not mean we have to run around in tongues all the time or that we even need to be speaking the prayers all the time. Remember God knows our thoughts so we can pray continuously talking to Him about everything. Prayer is what keeps our relationship strong with God and our trust in Him will grow as we stay in communication with Him. Think about it if we are not talking to our partner or our bosses at work, we would not have a very good relationship with them. Since we are Ambassadors for Christ, and we are doing the Work of the Lord then we cannot work and operate properly for Him without continued communication with Him. When we are praying for healings deliverance or provision, we need to make sure we are praying justly for God. This means that the prayers cannot have any I in them. Therefore, we have to stay repented so that we have no pride selfishness or self-righteousness in our prayers. Our thinking must change and the more we study the word and pray and stay in communication with God the more it will change. Jude 20 says, but ye beloved, building up yourself on your most holy faith, praying in the Holy Ghost. So now we are adding the shield of faith into our armor. But the faith he is talking about here is not just our own faith believing God can and will do things. The faith he is talking about here is the Gift of Faith. The God type faith. The kind of faith where we speak it and we know with no way or room for doubt that it is going to happen and God is going to move. Each person has a measure of faith, and we know that faith the size of a grain of mustard seed can move mountains but what this is talking about is the type of faith that comes with power and authority directly from the throne room of God. Continued fellowship with God, build our relationship with Him, and makes us more intimate which allows our faith to grow to that holy faith that Jude speaks of so we can put to work the gift of faith we already received when we received the Holy Ghost. Continued prayer will also make it easier for us to operate in the worship aspect of things.

Worship

There is a difference between singing along with songs and truly worshiping God. Really seeking Gods face and desiring to be in His tangible presence. Sometimes in order to gain full understanding of something we need to define what it is. Worship can be defined as an expression of reverence or adoration. Reverence is a deep respect. Respect is a deep feeling for someone elicited by their abilities and qualities or achievements. Adoration is a deep love or respect which creates in us a need to glorify and exalt that which we adore. Exalt means to place in high power over your life. Glorify means to acknowledge God's majesty. Worship brings us into the presence of God and in His presence no evil can come against us. His glory protects us from the attack of the enemy that is where we find our peace. It is in His presence that we find our salvation our deliverance and where we discover who we are in God. Worship cannot truly happen until we get honest with God about our condition and need for Him. That is why in John 4:21-24 Jesus told the Samarian woman that we must worship in spirit and in truth. Worship rids us of our religion and guides us into faith and brings us to peace. Worship is so important to God that He place it in the 10 commandments. Thou shalt have no other Gods before me. This means that we cannot place anything in our life before our worship and relationship with God. Learning how to worship with our own mouths and through the Holy Ghost is important because there is going to come a time when we will have no music to worship with. We must learn how to make a joyful noise unto the Lord. How to speak words of endearment to Him. We must learn to open our mouths up and thank you praise Him and magnify Him for His holiness. We must learn how to be like David. If we cannot practice worship in the house of God with our brothers and sisters in Christ, we will struggle and stumble to worship while we are not in the house. Trying to live life without the presence of God is like trying to paint a house without any paint. Worship brings us into the Holy of Holies where He can minister to us personally. When worship takes place as a body together the tangible presence of God comes into the house, and He ministers to us all at one time. It is in times of being in His presence that some breakthroughs and deliverances take place and only in His presence is where the battle can be won.

Application

We all know or knew most of this information and still struggled with things and the reason for that is because we had the knowledge in part and didn't understand how it all worked together. We can just get by and make it into the kingdom through repentance. We can manage to live a decent life and make it to heaven with repentance and prayer. Then there is the fulfilled life of the believer where we are applying the fullness of the word to our life's living in repentance, praying and fellowshipping with God like He is our best friend and all we must talk to, and worshiping Him as he is our Lord. The application of the armor activates the operation of the gifts of the spirit which is where we will find our healings, deliverance, and provision from God. We cannot just do it in part and expect to think that He is going to move. We have had the Holy Ghost for years and never fully understood how to operate Him. This is just a piece of understanding that is going to come. As we go through this scripture there will be a lesson on what is meant to be done with the scripture. Some are meant to be prayed and spoke to cause God to move. While some require action on our behalf to get God to move. Lastly some will require only our Faith in that God will do as we are asking Him to do. There is that three things again… Think it is starting to look less like a coincidence and more like it was divinely placed to be that way.

Healing Scriptures used in Prayer

Bleeding

Ezekiel 16:6 "And when I passed by thee, and saw thee polluted in thine own blood, I said unto thee when thou wast in thy blood Live; yea I said unto thee when thou wast in thy blood. Live." This scripture stops bleeding when prayed over a person who is bleeding from a wound.

Burns

Isaiah 43:2 "When thou passest through the waters, I will be with thee; and through the rivers, they shall not overflow thee; when thou walkest through fire, thou shalt not be burned; neither shall the flame kindle upon thee." Removes the string from a burn and begins healing process when prayed over the burn. You can also pray the story of Shadraq Meshaq and Abednego in the firey furnace and how God sent Christ into the furnace with them so that no harm came to them and that they would not even smell of smoke to remove the sting from a burn.

Sin Sickness

Jeremiah 17:14 Heal me, O Lord, and I shall be healed; save me and I shall be saved: for thou art my praise. Sickness brought on by sin. Repent and pray for this for healing.

Wounds from Battle

Jeremiah 30:17 For I will restore health unto thee, and I will heal thee of thy wounds, saith the Lord; because they called thee an Outcast, saying, This is Zion, whom no man seeketh after. This is to be prayed for healing when coming against enemy and you receive physical wounds during battle. This was spoke for the Israelites during the tribulation. These wounds were received as part of chastisement.

Wounds from Chastisement

Deuteronomy 32:39 See now that I, even I, am he, and there is no god with me; I kill, and I make alive; I wound, and I heal: neither is there any that can deliver out of my hand. At this time God had returned to Israel and had come against their enemies. He is telling them that He is there and that He will heal them and that it is in His power to kill or to make alive. He says that nothing can remove them from His hands. He is their healer and their deliverer all in one. Pray this prayer when you have been chastised by God and have suffered spiritual and or physical wounds from it.

2Chronicals 7:14 If my people which are called by my name, shall humble themselves, and pray and seek my face, and turn from their wicked ways; then will I hear from heaven, and will forgive their sin, and will heal their land. This prayer is for national healing but can be used for personal and body of Christ healing. If the church has fallen into sin then repent and He will move on behalf of the body and restore it to its original state.

Strength

Isaiah 40:29 He giveth power to the faint; and to them that have no might he increaseth, strength. Pray this word when you are feeling week in physical body and weak in spirit.

Healing for sickness caused by transgression and iniquity.

Isaiah 53:4-5 Surely, he hath borne our griefs and carried our sorrows; yet we did esteem him stricken, smitten of God, and afflicted. But He was wounded for our transgressions, he was bruised for our iniquities; the chastisement of our peace was upon him; and with his stripes we are healed. This scripture addresses all disease and sickness that is brought upon us through sin. By His stripes we are healed. It is already done He already paid the price for these sins, and we no longer must walk in sickness because of them.

Broken Hearted, Troubled, and Afflicted

Psalms 34:17-19 The righteous cry, and the Lord heareth, and delivereth them out of all their troubles. The Lord is nigh unto them that are of broken heart; and sayeth such as be of a contrite spirit. Many are the afflictions of the righteous; but the Lord delivereth him out of them all.

Affliction is a cause of persistent pain. Contrite is a remorseful spirit.

Depression

Psalms 30:10-11 Hear O Lordv and have mercy upon me; Lord, be thou my helper. Thou has turned for me my mourning into dancing; thou hast put off my sackcloth, and girded me with gladness. As many troubles and times change depression will try to set in and this is the scripture to pray for deliverance from that spirit.

Heart disease or problems

Psalms 73:26 My flesh and my heart faileth: but God is the strength of my heart, and my portion forever. Pray this over anybody or oneself who is suffering from heart conditions.

Require Action for Healing or Deliverance

Blood Issues

Matthew 9:20-22 And behold a woman, which was diseased with an issue of blood twelve years, came behind him, and touched the hem of his garment; For she said within herself, if I may but touch his garment, I shall be whole. But Jesus turned him about, and when he saw her he said, Daughter, be of good comfort; thy faith hath made the whole. And the woman was made whole from that hour. This scripture covers any blood infections such as Dysentery. The healing came from the woman's own faith in that even just touching His garment she would be made whole. This is what praying the prayer of faith means. To believe it as soon as you say it that it will happen. That type of faith requires God to move it is like you reached up into heaven and touched Jesus' garment with your own hand.

Mark 5:22- 34 gives an account of the same woman, but the issues were more vast with the blood. Mark states that the woman had the issue 12 years as Matthew does but added that she had suffered many things with many physicians and spent all she had only to be getting worse. Mark says that the fountain of her blood was dried up and that the issue of blood was a plague. This means the healing in this scripture can be for any blood disease, from infections of the blood, hemophilia, blood clotting disorders, leukemia ect...

Dumb and Deaf Spirit (ALL MENTAL HEALTH and Spirit of Suicide and Epilepsy)

Mark 9:17-28 And one of the multitude answered and said, Master, I have brought unto thee my son, which hath a dumb spirit; and wheresoever he taketh him, he teareth him: and he foameth, and gnasheth with his teeth, and pineth away; I spake to they disciples that they should cast him out; and they could not. He answereth him, and saith, O faithless generation, how long shall I be with you? How long shall I suffer you? Bring him unto me. And they brought him unto him; and when he saw him straight way the spirit tare him; and he fell on the ground and wallowed foaming. And he asked his father, How long is it ago since this came unto him? And he said of a child. And ofttimes it hath cast him into the fire, and into the waters to destroy him; but if thou canst do any thing, have compassion on us and help us. Jesus said unto him,

If thou canst believe, all things are possible to him that believeth. And straightway the father of the child cried out, and said with tears, Lord I believe; help thou mine unbelief. When Jesus saw that the people came running together, he rebuked the foul spirit saying unto him Thou dumb and deaf spirit, I charge thee, come out of him, and enter no more into him. And the spirit cried, and rent him sore, and came out of hi: and he was as one dead insomuch that many said, He is dead. But Jesus took him by the hand and lifted him up; and he arose.

This same story is in Luke 9:37-42 and Matthew 17:14-19. In Matthew it is called a lunatic. Jesus addresses the lack of faith and unbelief that is in the people who are there and those who tried to cast it out. The mans ability to believe and have a little faith was needed here. In Matthew the very next lesson from Jesus was faith of a grain of mustard seed. The disciples were unable to cast it out because they did not have enough faith and they had allowed unbelief to creep in. The mustard seed parable people take it and think it is meant as a small measure of faith. But 99% of all mustard seeds when they hit the ground will grow. The faith required to cast this spirit out requires that there be no doubt when speaking to it. The prayer that needs to be prayed needs to be exactly what Jesus spoke to the spirit and always command the spirit to leave in Jesus' name because without Jesus name we have no authority to cast the spirit out and it can attack you. In Mark when asked why Jesus explained that this requires much fasting and prayer. Through fasting and prayer our faith is made stronger, and unbelief becomes less of an issue to face. The fact that we will not know when we will encounter issues like this we need to stay fasted up and prayed up in order to be able to contend with them as need come to not allow the person to have to live with the spirit any longer than they already have for they may give way to the suicidal aspect of it before we get through our fast. The spirit knowing that you are preparing will be worse on the person in the wait.

Skin disorders

Mark 1:40-45 And there came a leper to him, beseeching him, and kneeling down to him, and saying unto him, If thou wilt, thou canst make me clean. And Jesus moved with compassion, put forth his hand, and touched him. And saith unto him I will; be thou clean. And soon as he had spoken, immediately the leprosy departed from him, and he was cleansed. And straitly charged him, and forthwith sent him away; and saith unto him, See thou say nothing to any man but go thy way, shew thyself to the priest, and offer for they cleansing those things which Moses commanded, for a testimony unto them. But he went out, and began to publish it much, and to blaze abroad the matter, insomuch that Jesus could no more openly enter the city but was without in desert places; and they came to him from every quarter. Jesus spoke to the man's skin to be clean then gave the man directives to give an offering to the Lord and to be quiet about what had happened. This was not a spirit it was a sin issue the man needed to be cleansed of generational sin to be healed. We must ask forgiveness of our fathers' sin to be healed of skin disorders. This covers all skin disfiguring disorders. Luke's account of it says Jesus laid hands on the man and spoke the cleansing over him so the laying on of hands and the gift of healing will be used for this to happen. Confess sins repent and lay hands on the person for the healing of the skin to take place.

Muscular Problems

Luke 5:17-24 And it came to pass on a certain day, as he was teaching, that there were Pharisees and doctors of the law sitting by, which we come out of every town of Galilee, and Judaea, and Jerusalem: and the power of the Lord was present to heal them. And behold, men brought in a bed a man which was taken with a palsy: and they sought means to bring him in, and to lay him before Him. And when they could not find by what way they might bring him in because of the multitude, they went upon the housetop, and let him down through the tiling with his couch into the midst before Jesus. And when he saw their faith, he said unto him, they sins are forgiven thee. And the scribers and the Pharisees began to reason, saying, who is this which speaketh blasphemies? Who can forgive sins but God alone? But when Jesus perceived their thoughts, he answering said unto them, What reason ye in your hearts? Whether is easier, to say Thy sins be forgiven thee; or to say, Rise up and walk? But that ye may know that the Son of Man hath power upon earth to forgive sins (he said unto the sick of palsy,) I say unto thee, Arise, and take up thy couch, and go into thine house. This healing was brought on by the faith of those who brought him to Jesus. Through their faith that Jesus could forgive sin and heal the man Jesus moved forgave his sin and healed his body of the affliction that was brought on him by the sin. This required action on their part to bring him to Jesus and to press in until they got to him by any means.

Disorders brought on by physical, mental and spiritual weakness.

Luke 13:11-13 And behold there was a woman which had a spirit of infirmity eighteen years, and was bowed together, and could in no wise lift up herself. And when Jesus saw her, he called her to him, and said unto her, Woman, thou art loosed from thine infirmity. And he laid his hands on her; and immediately she was made straight, and glorified God. This requires that we deal with the spirit of infirmity and then lay hands on the person and pray for healing. This is a spirit of bondage, and the person must be made loose from the bondage that has them crippled. When we are in a state that we are weak, whether internally or outwardly Satan can come upon us and put us in a bondage with a spirit of infirmity which attacks in our weakness. Jesus explains how this spirit works in verses 15-16. Spiritually and mentally these bondages will be sinful and require confession and repentance to be delivered from the bondage and for the spirit to be cast out.

Swelling and any disorder that has to do with it.

Luke 14:1-6 And it came to pass, as he went into the house of one of the chief Pharisees to eat bread on the sabbath da, that they watched him. And behold there was a certain man before him which had the dropsy (swelling). And Jesus answering spake unto the lawyers and Pharisees, saying, Is it lawful to heal on the sabbath day? And they held their peace. And he took him, and healed him and let him go; And answered them saying, which of you shall have an ass or an ox fallen into a pit, and will not straightway pull him out on the sabbath day? And they could not answer him again to these things. This healing was for a lesson to those who were watching him to see if He would violate the laws. Sometimes God will put people in our path and it is through our own faith and our belief that the healing will take place simply so that others will see and believe upon Him.

Blindness

John 9:1-7 And as Jesus passed by, he saw a man which was blind from his birth, And his disciples asked him, saying Master, who did sin, this man or his parents, that he was born blind? Jesus answered, Neither hath this man sinned, nor his parents; but that the works of God should be made manifest in him. I must work the works of him that send me, while it is day; the night cometh, when no man can work. As long as I am in the world, I am the light of the world. When he had thus spoken, he spat on the ground, and made clay of the spittle, and he anointed the eyes of the blind man with the clay, And said unto him Go wash in the pool of Siloam, (which is by interpretation Sent.) He went his way therefore, and washed, and came seeing. Sometimes blindness is brought on through sin and others it is meant only to be healed so God can be manifested in the persons life for them to believe upon being healed that and others also. He anointed his eyes with the spittle. It is through the anointing and the washing of the person that the healing took place. Anoint the eyes and baptize the person.

Deafness and Speech problems.

Mark 7:32-37 And the bring unto him one that was deaf, and had an impediment in his speech; and they beseech him to put hand upon him. And he took him aside from the multitude, and put his fingers into his ears, and he spit, and touched his tongue; and looking up to heaven sighed, and saith

31

unto him, Eph pha-tha, that is Be opened. And straightway his ears were opened, and the string of his tongue was loosed, and he spake plain. And he charged them that they should tell no man; but more he charged them, so much more a great deal they published it; And were beyond measure astonished, saying He hath done all things well; He maketh both the deaf to hear and the dumb to speak. Anoint the ears and the tongue and pray for God to open the ears and loose the tongue to speak. Luke 11:14 and Matthew 9:32-33 both refer to the dumb spirit being cause for people not being able to talk.

Sickness that creates and cause Fevers

Mark 1:29-34 And forthwith, when they were come out of the synagogue, they entered into the house of Simon and Andrew, with James and John, But Simons wife's mother lay sick of a fever, and anon they tell him of her. And he came and took her by the hand and lifted her up; and immediately the fever left her, and she ministered unto them. Lay hands on them for healing. This one was done through the anointing and the power of God only

other than laying on of hands there is nothing
required of anybody besides faith.

Raised the Dead

Luke 8:49-56 While he yet spake, there cometh
one from the ruler of the synagogue's house,
saying to him, Thy daughter is dead; trouble not
the Master. But when Jesus heard it he answered
him saying, Fear not; believe only, and she shall be
made whole. And when he came into the house, he
suffered no man to go in, save Peter, and James,
and John, and the father and the mother of the
maiden. And all wept, and bewailed her: but he
said, Weep not; she is not dead, but sleepeth. And
they laughed him to scorn, knowing that she was
dead. And he put them all out, and took her by the
hand, and called, saying Maid arise. And her spirit
came again, and she rose straightway: and he
commanded to give her meat. And her parents we
astonished: but he charged them that they should
tell no man what was done. John 11:1-44 gives a
same account of speaking to the dead to arise or
come forth and their spirit returns to their body and
they come back to life. Jesus told them to believe.
So we must believe and speak life back to the body

of the person who is dead. Follow the leading of the Holy Ghost on this.

Unclean Spirits (unnamed illnesses this is for the sicknesses and disease that are not listed above)

Matthew 10:1 And when he had called unto him these twelve disciples, he gave them power against unclean spirits, to cast them out, and to heal all manner of sickness and all manner of disease. The ability to cast out unclean spirits and to heal the sicknesses they caused was given to us as we were sent out to do the work. Mark 5:1-20 Legion was many unclean spirits.

Provision and Working of Faith and Worship

Tithes

Malachi 3:10-12 Bring ye all the tithes into the storehouse, that there may be meat in mine house, and prove me now herewith, saith the Lord of hosts, if I will not open you the windows of heaven, and pour you out a blessing, that there shall not be room enough to receive it. And I will rebuke the devourer for your sakes, and he shall not destroy the fruits of your ground; neither shall your vine cast her fruit before the time of the field, saith the Lord of hosts And all nations shall call you blessed: for ye shall be a delightsome land, saith the Lord of hosts. When we talk about tithes it comes as 10% of your first fruits. So anytime you receive for your labor you are to give 10% to God. This also include from your labor and harvest. But many forget to tithe there time to God. He gets 10% of your day. Two hours and 40 minutes a day belong to God. Either through prayer worship or fellowship. To not give him that time is the same as robbing from His house. Because we are the temple and not giving God his time within His temple is robbing him.

Shepard, Provider, and Protector

Psalms 23 The Lord is my shepherd; I shall not want. He maketh me to lie down in green pastures: he leadeth me beside the still waters. He restoreth my soul: he leadeth me in the paths of righteousness for his name's sake. Yea, though I walk through the valley of the shadow of death, I will fear no evil: for thou art with me; thy rod and thy staff they comfort me. Thou preparest a table before me in the presence of mine enemies: thou anointest my head with oil; my cup runneth over. Surely goodness and mercy shall follow me all the days of my life: and I will dwell in the house of the Lord forever. Speak this back to God in Prayer to see His hand move on your behalf in times of trouble, need, stress, guidance, when fear comes against you, and whenever you just need His presence to run over you for encouragement, courage, and peace.

Rain for crops to grow

Psalms 69:9 Thou, O God, didst send a plentiful rain, whereby thou didst confirm thine inheritance, when it was weary. Through times of drought there is need of rain for the plants to grow and produce needs. Prayer of faith with this scripture. Psalms

147:8 Who covereth the heaven with clouds, who prepareth rain for the earth, who maketh grass to grow upon the mountains. This is just another scripture to pray for rain.

Water

Numbers 20:1-13 Then came the children of Israel, even the whole congregation, into the desert of Zin in the first month: and the people abode in Kadesh; and Miriam died there and was buried there. And there was no water for the congregation: and they gathered themselves together against Moses and against Aaron. And the people chode with Moses, and spake, saying, Would God that we had died when our brethren died before the Lord! And why have ye brought up the congregation of the Lord into this wilderness, that we and our cattle should die there? And wherefore have ye made us to come up out of Egypt, to bring us in unto this evil place? it is no place of seed, or of figs, or of vines, or of pomegranates; neither is there any water to drink. And Moses and Aaron went from the presence of the assembly unto the door of the tabernacle of the congregation, and they fell upon their faces: and the glory of the Lord appeared unto them. And the Lord spake unto Moses, saying, Take the rod, and gather thou the assembly together, thou, and Aaron thy brother, and speak ye unto the rock before their eyes; and it shall give forth his water, and thou shalt bring forth to them water out of the rock: so thou shalt give the congregation and their beasts drink. And Moses took the rod from before the Lord, as he commanded him. And Moses and Aaron gathered the congregation together before the rock, and he said unto them, Hear now, ye rebels; must we fetch you water out of this rock? And Moses lifted up his hand, and with his rod he smote the rock twice: and the water came out abundantly, and the congregation drank, and their beasts also. And the Lord spake unto Moses and Aaron, because ye believed me not, to sanctify me in the eyes of the children of Israel, therefore ye shall not bring this congregation into the land which I have given them. This is the water of Meribah; because the children of Israel strove with the Lord, and he was sanctified in them. God will provide water for drinking and with sanctification in it if we are in need and seek His face for it.

Physical needs as you come in need of them

Matthew 6:25-34 Therefore I say unto you, Take no thought for your life, what ye shall eat, or what ye shall drink; nor yet for your body, what ye shall put on. Is not the life more than meat, and the body than raiment? Behold the fowls of the air: for they sow not, neither do they reap, nor gather into barns; yet your heavenly Father feedeth them. Are ye not much better than they? Which of you by taking thought can add one cubit unto his stature? And why take ye thought for raiment? Consider the lilies of the field, how they grow; they toil ot, neither do they spin: And yet I say unto you, That even Solomon in all his glory was not arrayed like one of these. Wherefore, if God so clothe the grass of the field, which today is, and tomorrow is cast into the oven, shall he not much more clothe you, O ye of little faith? Therefore take no thought, saying, What shall we eat? or, What shall we drink? or, Wherewithal shall we be clothed? (For after all these things do the Gentiles seek:) for your heavenly Father knoweth that ye have need of all these things. But seek ye first the kingdom of God, and his righteousness; and all these things shall be added unto you. Take therefore no thought for the morrow: for the morrow shall take thought for the things of itself. Sufficient unto the day is the evil thereof. The most important part of all this scripture is the part where we are told to seek ye first the kingdom of heaven. This means to seek after the things of God first and for His kingdom first. In order for this scripture to be applied it literally requires us to be selfless and be worried more for others and their needs. God will honor us trying to provide and help further His kingdom by taking care of our needs.

Philippians 4:19 But my God shall supply all your need according to his riches in glory by Christ Jesus. Another scripture to pray and speak in time of need.

Spiritual Needs

2 Peter 1:3 According as his divine power hath given unto us all things that pertain unto life and godliness, through the knowledge of him that hath called us to glory and virtue: Through His word and spirit all things we need to live in godliness are provided to us. We can find all we need in the word of God and guidance for how to use it and what needs to be done through His spirit.

Power

Acts 2:17-18 And it shall come to pass in the last days, saith God, I will pour out of my Spirit upon all flesh: and your sons and your daughters shall prophesy, and your young men shall see visions, and your old men shall dream dreams: And on my servants and on my handmaidens I will pour out in those days of my Spirit; and they shall prophesy: Often we think this is just about the church but he said all flesh and those who are filled and receive it will receive power from on high and will operate in all the gifts of the spirit as there is need of them.

1Corinthians 12:7-10 But the manifestation of the Spirit is given to every man to profit withal. For to one is given by the Spirit the word of wisdom; to another the word of knowledge by the same Spirit; To another faith by the same Spirit; to another the gifts of healing by the same Spirit; To another the working of miracles; to another prophecy; to another discerning of spirits; to another divers kinds of tongues; to another the interpretation of tongues: Upon being filled with the spirit we receive all the gifts and they operate through us as there is need of them. So as we encounter each of these things listed above God will be faithful to manifest the gift needed to operate accordingly as we need them.

Conclusion

As we enter a new exciting and different time with the Lord it is important that we stay focused on Him, His Kingdom, and doing His work. We will soon see these things needed and we need to stay continued in study and keeping ourselves sharped to what God is doing.

Made in the USA
Columbia, SC
28 September 2024

42514639R00026